Peepers
the
Talking Starling

and
A Better World

Written By Judi Willkins Sarkisian
Illustrated By Clifford Smith

This book is a work of non-fiction. Names and places have been changed to protect the privacy of all individuals. The events and situations are true.

ISBN: 978-1-4140-3092-0 (sc)
ISBN: 978-1-4140-3093-7 (hc)
ISBN: 978-1-4140-3094-4 (e)

Library of Congress Control Number: 2003098555

Print information available on the last page.

This book is printed on acid-free paper.

1stBooks – rev. 10/26/2021

Peepers the Talking Starling
A bird's eye view of A Better World.

With special thanks to photographers Rick Rainey and Ruth Dayes who documented the Peepers' story as it happened. Thank you to all the singer/songwriters like Joe Rathburn, Deborah Liv Johnson and Delene St. Clair whose songs inspired Peepers to talk. Many thanks to all the musicians like Jeff Pekarek, dancers like Beatriz Basile and artists like Michael Leas who performed through Peepers screeching, ducked from flying objects and gave this story artistic credibility. Thank you friends, thank you family, we couldn't do any of this without you!!

Judi Sarkisian
Clifford Smith

Dedication

This book is dedicated to all the people who have taken the time and the interest to try and make the world a better place. Sometimes it is writing a song or poem, painting a picture or preparing a wonderful meal. Other times it is as grand as building a business, being involved in the political and social systems that govern us or taking on the task of teaching what is good. It can be as simple as planting a tree, saving a bird or helping your neighbor.

Each day there are opportunities for us to love, to learn and to be awed. In a world that many times rewards greed, selfishness and the distortion of the truth, it is important to recognize and fulfill those opportunities to do what is better. As we connect life-to-life, mind-to-mind and spirit-to-spirit, we will be able to walk on the path of truth and love together. Our walk through A Better World was filled with magical, inspiring and memorable experiences, created by the performers, artists and pets who came our way. We will be forever grateful for their gifts.

Judi and Jim

In memory of Frank McClelland

It was Monday morning, the shop and restaurant owners on Goldfinch Street were cleaning up from the weekend and getting ready for the new week. Delivery trucks were making their stops at the restaurants: dropping off supplies of paper goods, produce, fresh fish and all of the other necessary ingredients for business.

Goldfinch Street is a popular destination for hungry people, thirsty people, tired people and those who just like to enjoy a pleasant environment.

Judi and Jim owned *A Better World*, a bookstore and performance space that provided refreshments, information, comfort and entertainment to its many visitors. Jim spent most of his time being an orthopedic surgeon, while Judi put on the different hats of manager, promoter, owner and slave. Even on a Monday morning, Judi liked the welcome of the large open doors, the inviting patios, the smell of coffee and cinnamon rolls.

But this morning her thoughts were rudely shattered!

"Peep. Pe-e-e-p, Pe-e-e-e-p."

Judi looked around. What could possibly be making that horrible shrieking sound? Then she saw the tiny little bird struggling to walk right in the doorway of *A Better World*.

No bigger than a chicken egg, it was a few stiff feathers, with a great big yellow beak wide open and yelling for all it was worth. Its little legs were all entwined in hair and twine and it kept falling over.

3

Judi picked it up gently and unwrapped its little feet, "Hey little one, what are you doing here?"

She had seen a less fortunate baby bird in the street the day before and thought there was probably a nest in the big sign for the TV store next door. She put the baby bird in a box under a tree in hopes that the Mama bird would hear the baby and come and feed it.

Every hour Judi went out and checked on the baby bird, and every hour its PEEPS got louder. Finally, Judi brought it into her office and tried to find a phone number for a local wildlife rescue agency. Lots of phone numbers, but only recordings or busy signals. The day was pressing on and Judi had a lot of things to attend to for the evening performance. "Might as well feed you little one, until I can figure out where to take you."

Judi went across the street to The Gathering restaurant and asked the owner, Dan, for some hamburger to feed the baby bird. It was the closest thing Judi could think of that might taste like worms to a baby bird. She found some tweezers and an eyedropper and set about with water and hamburger trying to quiet the baby bird down. It worked! In a little while the baby was asleep and Judi was able to get on to her work. But that didn't last long! In 2 hours, just like with any other baby, the bird was PEEPING. This wasn't going to be easy!

Donna is a local actress who worked as Judi's assistant when she wasn't in a play or making movies. She had found the baby bird the day before and had also tried to get it back to its bird family. She was watching the care of the baby bird with an "oh-oh, here it comes," look. She was right, her job description was expanded to baby bird feeding. Soon she and Judi were working around the clock to keep the **PEEPing** baby bird quiet.

A Better World was open almost 24 hours a day, so it wasn't very difficult to keep the little bird fed. The hard part was keeping it from waking up and **PEEPing** during a performance. It did not matter where they moved the little bird's box, you could hear it everywhere. Most of the time Peepers was kept in the loft that served as Judi's office. The performance space and a grand stage were below the office. There were several performances every night of the week, everything from guitar concerts to flamenco dance shows and late night comedy acts. Judi knew the Monday night "opera" crowd would not appreciate the peeping newcomer.

7

During the day, the office was a constant stream of phone calls and visitors as the events and performances were planned and put into production. Judi probably answered the phone at least 50 times a day, *"A Better World*, this is Judi, may I help you."* Not to mention all of the intercom calls from the café, bookstore and boutique employees.

The days went by and the little bird grew feathers, beautiful dark feathers with white star-like dots on the ends of the feathers. Judi carried the baby bird around with her in a shoebox; it was easier than going from one end of the space to the other for feeding times. She bought the baby bird a beautiful cage to sleep in at night and found it would stay pretty quiet when it was covered.

Everyday Judi meant to find the wildlife rescue people, certainly before the bird began to fly. That day came without much warning. Judi had put a mixture of cat food and crackers down on her desk for Peepers, who could now eat very well on his own. Peepers ate, tore a few papers on Judi's desk and took off FLYING over the performance space.

Judi ran down the stairs and called to everyone "look our Peepers is flying."

The interior of the building was in a large circle with open doors and two story ceilings. It was beautiful to see that little bird swoop and fly. All the people in the café ducked as Peepers flew over their heads. Judi thought for sure Peepers would just fly out the front doors. But Peepers had other ideas and flew back to land on Judi's head.

Well, this presented an immediate problem. Judi called a friend at the zoo, to see if they knew who would take this little bird and help it prepare for the outdoor world. They gave her the phone number for Project Wildlife. Judi dialed the number and waited through the recording. Peepers was sitting on her arm, pulling on the hairs. Such a beautiful little bird.

Then Judi heard her phone ring. That couldn't be, she was on the phone. It rang again and she heard it being picked up and a voice said, "*A Better World,* this is Judi, may I help you?" Judi dropped the phone in disbelief; she must be working too hard. There is no way that little bird could have said what she thought it said. But Peepers obviously was not planning on leaving *A Better World,* and repeated his greeting again, along with a few laughs that were unmistakably familiar to Judi.

11

Judi could not possibly let a bird who talked and liked to ride on people's heads fend for itself in the outside world. *A Better World* had its new mascot. A customer, who knew more about birds than Judi, identified Peepers as a European Starling. The starling is related to blackbirds and mynah birds, so its talent at mimicry is understandable.

Over the years there were many funny Peepers stories. Peepers became a star in his own right. Neighborhood children dropped by everyday to hear him say, "I love you, give me a kiss," as he flew down and landed on their head or on their finger. But the story that Judi loved to tell the best was the day that Peepers met the "Jaws of Life!"

It was a beautiful Sunday afternoon, a 4:00 classical guitar concert was scheduled with classical guitarists Fred Benedetti and George Svoboda. They were regular performers at A Better World and always had a large audience. They also were used to the antics of Peepers and had included the bird in more than one of their shows.

People were coming in and the performers were setting up their equipment. Judi let Peepers fly around one more time and then called him to go in his cage. But this day Peepers decided to be difficult and kept flying everywhere except into his cage. Hopping just out of Judi's reach Peepers managed to catch his foot in the grillwork on top of her computer. Judi frantically tryed to unhook a hysterical Peepers from the computer. But little Peepers was starting to go limp from fright. Judi screamed for help. Guitarists and audience members scrambled to her aid. Everyone had an idea of how to rescue Peepers, but nothing worked. In one last tearful plea, Judi sent for the neighborhood firemen to bring the "Jaws of Life." She would crush the computer if she must, but Peepers would lose neither life or limb.

The firehouse was less than a block away and in minutes, several firefighters arrived in their yellow slickers, with the "Jaws of Life" and other life-saving props. Their message had been that someone was trapped and needed rescuing immediately at *A Better World*.

Up the stairs they raced ready for anything. Peepers took one look at the firefighters with the "Jaws of Life" and shrieked "talk to you later, bye now!" He pulled his little foot free and flew into his cage.

Judi was very grateful for the firefighters. She was sure Peepers thought that they were four very large yellow birds coming to get him and he had better rescue himself!

Judi gave the firemen brownies and cookies to take back to the fire station. And in a few moments, almost like nothing had happened, the guitar concert began and everyone settled in to a musical afternoon at *A Better World*.

Peepers' vocabulary continued to grow. He mimicked all the employees, voices over the phone, the sounds of equipment, and could book a show almost as well as Judi. The only thing Peepers couldn't mimic was music. He could not carry a tune at all. Donna tried and tried to teach Peepers to whistle, but after one note, it was a garbled screeching mess. Maybe it was just as well, Peepers was already stealing the show from a lot of performers. At least the musicians were safe!

Jim's favorite Peepers story involved a customer who had irritated him for years.

The woman only came to the free events and would ask for lemon and sugar with her free water and wanted to make sure the water was filtered. She would read all the magazines and never bought one, complaining if the latest issue had not arrived. She would bring food from a fast-food restaurant to eat on the patio and snarled at everyone. During a summer performance the air conditioner was pumping away and the place was packed. Ms. Grumpy called to Jim as he put out some more chairs. "What's the matter with your air conditioner it's hot in here." People around her suggested she take off her sweater and coat. She just glowered and yelled out again "Hey get me one of those fans you have upstairs."

Jim turned red and bit his tongue. Judi was always lecturing him on "the customer is always right." Then, from Judi's office, Peepers swooped down over the stage heading straight for Ms. Grumpy. Ms. Grumpy shrieked, waving her arms, "I hate birds, get it away from me." Peepers persevered and like a mocking bird dived for the lady, stopping in flight just long enough to leave a big deposit on her shoulder.

The lady shook her fist at Jim. "If you don't get rid of that bird I'm never coming back!" Peepers flew to Jim's shoulder laughing loudly. The audience roared with laughter, the lady had her answer and Jim got his wish.

Judi and Jim decided to close *A Better World* and focus on some other projects. It had been a difficult decision, mainly because they were very worried about how Peepers would take the move to their home. This was a home with other birds, cats and dogs. Lots of competition and not as much freedom for Peepers.

Judi and Jim, had decided to give Peepers the upstairs, where he would be safe from the cats, who preferred the downstairs. He would be able to fly free part of the time and be with Judi and Jim all of the time. With a lot of preparation they brought Peepers to his new home. Peepers loved to sit on Judi's hand, so Judi took him out of his cage to reassure him that everything would be OK. Just at that moment, Jim opened the downstairs front door. In a flash, Peepers flew through the upstairs rooms, swooped down the stairs and out the door.

Judi and Jim were devastated. They were worried that Peepers would try to fly back to *A Better World*. They went up and down the street calling for Peepers. Tearfully, they set his cage outside, hoping he would find it. They called the employees at *A Better World* to open the front doors, just in case he found his way back. With no sight or word of Peepers, Judi and Jim walked back into the house. Swoosh; flying in beside them was their darling starling! Peepers had been sitting in a tree near the door watching the whole show!

Never again did Peepers fly out the door. Outside never had held an attraction for him. He had everything he wanted with Judi and Jim.

In just a few days, Peepers adapted to his new home. He had a new cage at the head of Jim and Judi's bed and a large one out by the computer in the office. He would fly between cages and continued to impress visitors with conversations that seemed to be just for them!

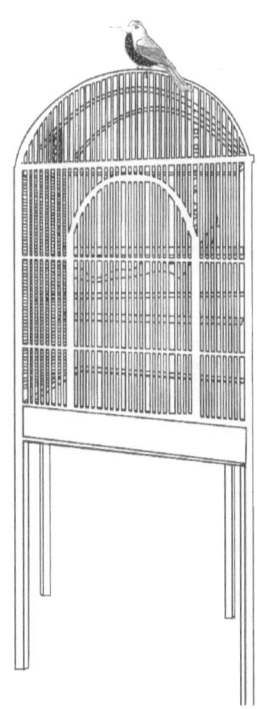

He was happier than ever because he had Judi and Jim's attention almost 24 hours a day!

More Orphans!

Now that Judi had more time, she returned to one of her favorite activities, raising orphan kittens. Before A Better World, she had worked with a local agency, Friends of Cats. She eagerly signed up for their foster care program.

Peepers was very attentive to the nursing process and would sit on Judi's hand while she fed the baby kittens. Of course just like Peepers had, babies grow up. But Peepers made it very clear who the boss was. Peepers would herd all the kittens into a group by pecking at their toes. (Starlings love to peck and look between things like toes). Then once the kittens were corralled, Peepers would march up and down in front of them like a drill sergeant, lecturing them on the finer points of life.

Left over form his days at *A Better World*, Peepers had a large crystal bowl for bathing more than one customer had looked for a rain cloud as they were splashed by Peepers' bath from Judi's loft. Every thing in Judi's office had been anointed by Peeper's bath water.

Peepers liked to wait until the kittens were gathered around for a drink, then splash down in the middle of the bowl sending kittens scurrying in all directions.

There was always that day when a kitten would decide to chase Peepers. But Peepers would just fly high and laugh! Foster kittens move on to their permanent homes when they are quite young, so Peepers always remained The Boss!

Saying Good-Bye

Peepers grew older and flew less and less. The stars disappeared on his feathers and he was very happy to just sit on Judi and let her carry him around. But he would still surprise everyone with a new phrase. More than once, Judi sat red-faced as Peepers imitated her saying something that should not be repeated!

Peepers left Judi and Jim's life as quickly as he came into it. He had been talking and laughing and just stopped. As fans found out that Peepers had died, there were many letters and cards. Peepers had touched the lives of many in a very special way. Even today, People love to recall the talking starling from A Better World. As they tell their stories, there is a connection, heart to heart. And they are grateful for their good fortune to have known Peepers, the talking starling.

Peeper's
Enduring Memories
and
Fan Letters

PHOTO BY
Ruth Dayes

IN MEMORY
of
PEEPERS

We knew it would happen some day,
but that day was always far far away in our hearts.
On September 28, 1999, Peepers took the forever flight in the sky.

Our hearts have a huge empty place,
but our memories are alive and a great comfort.
Peepers personally introduced Jim and I to the amazing world of
intelligence, consciousness and emotion existing in the wild animal kingdom.

That connection has lead us to a greater commitment to
continued research in communication between animals and humans.

To honor the memory of Peepers we are asking all of you who knew him
to send us your favorite story about meeting Peeps or hanging out with him.

We are going to publish those stories in a book for all of us
to have as reminder of the good things that happened at A Better World

Thank you so much for being a part of Peepers' life.
Thank you for being a part of our life.

Judi & Jim

There are certain indomitable creatures who possess such a magnitude of spirit and will to survive that their existence cannot be denied-attention must be paid. Perhaps surpassing the fate nature had originally intended, Peeps was such a creature. Alternately known as Peeps, Peepers and Ms. Peeps (to this day, I'm uncertain of Peeps' sex) I'm sure she's chattering and whistling away in animal paradise, providing entertainment for all life forms. From the time she, literally, hopped into the café at "A Better World," it was clear that Peeps was meant not only to survive, but thrive in a world of adoring humans. Full of surprises, she served to affirm the inexplicable bonds that connect the kingdoms of life.

Peeps was re-born the day she fell from a tree. Inhabiting a nest with a less hardy sibling who couldn't survive such an early life trauma, Peeps persisted, insisting and demanding that her existence on planet earth continue. Respectful of her spunk and determination, I did what any decent, caring, clueless animal lover (albeit not a "bird person") would do. I set up a box complete with towel and birdseed (which, in her featherless condition, she had no hope of being able to eat) and set her outside for her wayward mother to come and retrieve her.

Arriving for work the next day, I discovered Peeps had once again been rescued from peril. Judi had found her outside the door entrapped by pieces of string, struggling to be free. Judi, being a more experienced Florence Nightingale than I, nurtured Peeps with eyedroppers of sugar water and a warm and toasty, towel-lined Xerox box set up in the back storage room. With barely a feather to call her own, Peeps was fed by employees in shifts around the clock. More than a bird, Peeps became a loving friend to all who knew her, a special gift from the animal world to come share its secrets and treasures with oblivious humans.

After attempting to place her with various animal rescue organizations, it became clear that Peeps was here to stay, a new mascot. Peeps settled nicely into domesticated life, unusual in itself for a wild starling. Little did we know what strange and rare talents were yet to be revealed.

I don't remember exactly what she said initially, but I clearly remember the first time I heard her say it. Judi, on occasion prone to embellishment, insisted that Peeps spoke to her. "Oh, that's nice, she sure did." (Senora esta un poquito loco en la cabeza.) Quite frankly, we humored her, until one day, as I was sitting in the upstairs office working on press releases, a disembodied voice, as if from an alien, otherworldly spirit spoke, clear as a bell, perfectly mimicking Judi's voice. *"A Better World*, this is Judi, may I help you?"* Whereupon I rushed downstairs and told some of the other employees that Peeps did, in fact, speak. "Sure she did, that's nice." (Senora esta un poquito loco en la cabeza.) Gradually, they all came to discover Peeps' extraordinary talents.

Steadily expanding her verbal repertoire, the legend and wonder of Peeps spread far and wide. A perfect mimic, gleefully providing both sides of the conversation, including foreign accents, pauses, sighs and inflections of exclamations and surprise. Chattering away during concerts, I even had a patron once ask me if I could turn down the answering machine in the office while the concert was going on. I diligently tried to explain that I wasn't able to, as it wasn't a machine, it was Peeps.

I have long since learned more about earthworms and mealworms than I ever wanted to know. I learned to constantly have a towel slung over my shoulder to avoid Peeps little souvenir droppings. I regret to say that Peeps learned an expletive or two from me. "Jesus Christ, Peeps. God damn it!" as another shirt received an excremental blessing.

Peeps lead a rich, full life making our lives richer and fuller in the process. She will be missed, undoubtedly, but never forgotten; an indelible imprint on our hearts remains, along with her irreplaceable spirit.

Donna Walker is a local actress. In between theatre and television appearances she lent her talent and extraordinary professional expertise to A Better World. She currently resides is Los Angeles, furthering her acting career.

I usually stopped by *A Better World* on Friday evenings after work, to visit Judi and Jim and enjoy the atmosphere of A Better World. Judi was often busy with customers and performers and I enjoyed quietly reading in her loft/office listening to the many happy sounds of the café and bookstore. Peeps' cage was in the loft.

One evening, I heard what sounded like the telephone ringing, only it wasn't. Then I heard what sounded like Judi answering the phone, *"Better World*, this is Judi, may I help you?" But Judi wasn't there. I looked up to see Peeps happily making telephone ringing sounds, then answering the phone in Judi's voice and carrying on a conversation using phrases Judi would normally use. It was quite astonishing.

Susan Drake is Judi's sister. She is now retired from her job with the City of San Diego. She continues to give loving support to her sister's ongoing projects in the arts.

One afternoon, while I was preparing for a show that night at *A Better World*, I sat upstairs in Judi's office replacing my guitar strings and warming up. Peeps was there with me in his cage and chattering away making normal starling sounds. Whenever I'd sing or play, he would become more animated until I heard "Thank you for calling *A Better World.* This is Judi, may I help you?" I was blown away by this bird's perfect imitation of Judi doing her phone routine, one it must have heard a thousand times as it sat there in her office day after day. This was when I first realized that a starling was capable of mimicry and I was shocked, and thoroughly charmed as well. Peeps was an amazing bird, I think though that he wouldn't have amounted to as much without the care and companionship he received at the hands of Judi and Jim. There was a perfect symbiosis (as well as a little magic) there.

Judi & Jim

I was very saddened when I got your memorial letter. I sure wish I could have experienced Peeps once more. My heart goes out to you both for your loss. We'll have to get together soon and toast to Peepers! Would coming over to our new house for dinner sometime in the near future be of interest to you two?

Love,
Joe

Joe Rathburn is one of San Diego's leading singer/songwriters. Visit him at his web page www.joerathburn.com and catch one of his local concerts.

Hi Judi & Jim,

I was so sad to hear that Peepers passed on to the great bird nest in the sky. Did he live out a normal birdie life span? I have no idea how long starlings live, but he certainly brought happiness to a lot of people for the time he was here.

The first time Judi brought Peeps downstairs at the *Better World* to show me, I must admit I was a little skeptical of a talking starling. After all, we hear about talking African Greys and Myna birds, but a starling?! Well now, come to think of it, I think I DID hear an extra telephone ringing upstairs at the *Better World* every now and then when I'd be performing there!

So When Judi brought Peeps downstairs, he was a little quiet — at first. So, we gave up trying to coax some sounds out of him. He sat quietly on my shoulder and Judi and I talked for a while. Well, I guess Peeps couldn't stand being left out of the conversation, so he jumped right in! First the famous telephone ring that he imitates so impeccably, followed by "Judi's" cheery talking. In fact I thought she had learned to be a darned good ventriloquist! Well, this was just the beginning of the conversation. He went on and on with all sorts of voice imitations of practically everyone that works at the *Better World*, and every phone ring, and even voices as they sound through the intercom, which has kind of a funny echo to it. WOW! I was impressed. I've never heard a bird talk so well even at the zoo shows! After that, I was telling everyone that starlings can be taught to talk, and everyone was very surprised.

I love starlings anyway. I love to hear a whole flock of them chirp in the trees, because it reminds me of my childhood days and the huge trees where they used to sing all day long.

Peepers indeed brought many people a sense of wonder and a special connection with the animal world. He was a gentle little birdie whom we will all miss—a darling starling named "Peepers"!

Love,
Delene

Delene St. Clair and her husband Barry Cahill have a great group called Hot Pursuit Band. They are still in touch with Judi and Jim, sharing more animal and musical moments.

Visit them at
www.hotpursuitmusic.com.

Lauren Liefland, Ph.D.

Dear Judi,

Carianna and I miss you and the Better World very, very much. That place was a real part of our lives and there hasn't been anything to fill the void that it's closing has left. Carianna knew it right away when she was told it would be closed. For me it came more gradually and we still talk about your Better World and how we would go a couple times a week. That's where Carianna first heard Flamenco and East European Klezmer music (thanks to your son). We still feel the loss, and thank you so much for the years you gave us that wonderful haven in Mission Hills.

As far as Peepers goes, one little memory was of Carianna and me waiting at the bottom of the stairs thinking that you were on the phone. Carianna wanted to say hello but I didn't want to interrupt if you were busy. It turned out it was Peepers saying, "Hello this is the Better World" and a couple of other phrases that sounded just like you!!

I am teaching a course in Child Development next month, and in preparing for it I was taping some documentary about animal intelligence and talking to Carianna about the fact that some scientists treat animals as if they can't feel or think. I told her they used to say what distinguished humans was our use of tools. Then that wonderful British naturalist reported her observation of chimpanzees making tools to eat ants. And dolphins have their own communication vocabulary, and it goes on and on. Of course they have emotions and complex intelligence! How arrogant of humans to treat them as if they don't! Bless you Judi. We love you.

51

Best wishes for the Year of the Dragon, Lauren

Lauren Leifman will always hold a special place in *A Better World* Memories. Not only is she a talented folk singer, she spent many hours in the coffee shop working on her Ph.D. Jim and Judi felt like proud "parents" when she received her doctorate degree. Her daughter, Carianna, added a special sense of family. Her awe and joy over the new experiences of the performing arts will always be remembered.

Dear Jim & Judi

There are so many wonderful stories I remember about Peepers, it was difficult to choose. Here is a couple that stand out in my memory! Never a day goes by that I don't remember Better World and everyone and everything in it. It was a magic time, I am so glad I was there. I wish we could have it all again. Being close to you and all creatures great and small is also A Better World. Love you both and hope to see you soon.

Love Doreen

Peepers to the Rescue

It was a hectic morning for me that day. I arrived at work not feeling too well but anxious to rearrange the jewelry cases in the boutique. I, then, heard a loud crash and realized the top glass shelf had fallen and glass was everywhere. I managed to sort things out and after an hour, was asked by a consigner to inventory all her merchandise- Whoopee!! I preceded upstairs to Judi's office to locate the records. By this time my head was aching and a cold was starting to blossom. When I reached the office Peepers, who was still in his cage, looked at me and said, "I love you, give me a kiss." Suddenly the head stopped aching and I was so glad to be at work at *Better World*-Thank you Peepers, I think you know what I needed. I love you!!

One afternoon, as I was walking downstairs at *Better World* I heard unfamiliar noises up in Judi's office. Rushing upstairs I found Judi hunched over the computer holding something and looking terrified. Donna, our secretary, said, Peepers has jammed his foot into the computer keyboard and she can't get it loose." Not knowing what to do I asked one of the girls at the café to go and ask the firemen at the station a couple of blocks away for advice. Soon one of the firemen arrived, carrying numerous pieces of equipment, and went up to the scene of the mishap. A few minutes later he passed through the boutique. "What happened, I asked."

"Need more cutting tools," he said.

"Oh please," I said, "Not Peepers foot."

"No," he replied, "for the computer."

By this time everyone around was concerned about Peepers, customer and employees. He came back with what looked like the" jaws of life," but was back in a few minutes. "Please," I said, "Don't tell me Peepers has expired."

"You won't believe this but that bird suddenly just pulled his foot out all by himself, he's fine but I think Judi and all of you need help."

What a wonderful creature.

Doreen Donnally is an employee, neighbor and a friend. A woman of timeless beauty, she has enhanced many Mission Hills boutiques with her expertise in sales and customer service. She always made *A Better World* look better!

Michael Leas

Hello Jim and Judi,

To start this story I want to relate I had the opportunity to be one of the many artists to show my work at the Better World Galleria. This brought great joy and direction to my life.

One day while I was at the Galleria I noticed a bird fluttering around. At first I thought that it had trapped itself by flying into the wrong place at the wrong time. From time to time out at the warehouse shop where I work there are birds that get trapped. I felt this was one of those cases. However in short time Judy asked me if I had seen "Peepers." What? I wondered. She said it was a bird she was nursing back to life. Cool, I thought, this place is made of all the right stuff. It brought to me a sense of nature here and now. So many times in this hustle and bustle world we lose sight of the beauty of all creatures great and small. Even the little brown, black birds play their role in expressing life. So that day went on and I went home not giving this event much thought. I did return time and time again to the Better World to catch one of the many shows, to study and hang out, meet new people, feel the essence of aliveness by fitting in.

On another day while doing some of the paperwork that needs to be done for the records, Peepers had landed on my shoulder. I have always loved birds and today would be the day I was tested to see how much I could LOVE all creatures. Peepers had pooped on my shoulder. It caught me by surprise and was a funny touch of "in the moment humor" that makes the soul chuckle and laugh with glee. I needed that for I have been one who has been so caught up in the seriousness of life too much and this helped to shatter this heavy feeling. Yes, birds of a feather flock together. The whole experience of the *Better World* helped me to break out of my shell and grow my wings and fly.

Across the Sea, across the skies
A breath of light whispered to my
ears and eyes
A sight to behold and a sight to see
It's a time for love and a time to be
free

I give to you and you give to me
I receive from you an eternity
A feeling of trust, a feeling of love
A peace within from the worlds above

(Chorus)
The feathered wings of freedom has
Set forth her breath
Be free, oh eternal spirit
Be free, and you'll never fear it
Be free, and you will always hear it
Freedom, sweet freedom

If you ever feel you can't go on
The ocean's too wide
The winds are too strong
You knock and see what's inside
You are searching for an open door
to life

Know you'll find what you need
By searching inside
Spread your wings and be free
The freedom to love, to share and
care
A power of measure beyond compare

(Repeat chorus)

Michael Leas is a visionary artist who graced the walls of *A Better World* with his inspiring and provocative art work. His life is dedicated to higher principles of spirituality and goodness. Visit him at his web site www.moonfeather.org.

Judi and Jim,

This is the funniest story I can report on Miss Peeps…

A patron is pondering on the decision to buy a very exciting necklace of Harold Swen. She was holding an amulet, when Miss Peeps arrives at her shoulder, almost scaring the hell out of her. Not knowing if it was a good omen or not, she took two days to decide whether or not to make the purchase. Finally Miss Peeps won out, she returned and bought the necklace.

Quentin owned the exotic boutique and antique stores "Ideas Incorporated". He is a clothing designer, a furniture designer and a man of great taste.

Dear Judi,

It was with great sadness and difficulty that I read your letter about Peeps. That was a hard one to digest! My heart can only guess at how you felt and have been feeling.

Peeps held a symbolic existence for me since she walked into *A Better World* about the same time that I did. We both met a golden angel who interceded in our lives out of pure kindness.

I have been witness to your giving of monies, jobs, food, and more. Dylan and I have also been the fortunate recipients of such, but I never bore witness more than that of your giving of love!!

My favorite story about Peeps is when you called me to say that Peeps was saying, "Mary, take a vacation. Mary needs a vacation." Boy did I ever!!

There are so many memories of Peeps for me. Her flying around the stage area, sitting on the computer monitor staring and talking to me, Peeps lying on your chest as if a love form extension, Peeps flying over surprised customers heads, children climbing those stairs just to see Peeps because they heard about him in the community. And last, but not at all the least, Peeps Poop, and did you ever stay on top of that! You're the greatest Judi!

I love you so very much. I treasure your friendship. I will remember Peeps and speak of the story and magic created by one little bird that walked into Judi's place one day. Peeps was no fool!

Love, Mary

Mary is a television producer, writer and developer of many media projects. She and her son Dylan were an important part of the *Better World* family.

Esther Cornell

Still Peepers

We're losers and weepers,
We really miss you Peepers.
Your flight was a great sight.
Now you've soared to a new height.
We won't ever forget you,
You're just out of our sight.
But your memory is still here,
Even though you're not near.

Esther is a graphic artist and superb calligrapher. Her elegant style has defined many articles as well as herself.

Barbara Wiese

For many years, I enjoyed doing psychic readings at *A Better World* Galleria. One Friday evening I had a question for Donna and found it necessary to go upstairs into the office section of the Galleria to find her. When I arrived upstairs, immediately Peepers landed on my head. What a surprise! Never before and never since, have I had a bird on my head. I stayed in the office until Peepers decided to fly away and with my question answered, I returned downstairs. It was an amazing experience and one that will always remain in the memories of my mind.

Barbara is a woman of many talents and many faces. An executive in the hotel industry, she is a matriarch in the corporate structure. Yet she can also hold the hand of a seeker and give them guidance into the intuitive world of self.

I Finally Meet **THE BIRD**,

I had heard stories about "Judi Willkin's little bird, Miss Peeps" before I ever saw "her". Though she hadn't been around for long, she already had quite a reputation among the poets and musicians who frequented *A Better World*. But the first time I really got a look at her, I admit that I was entirely under whelmed. I had dropped by A Better World without an appointment — a sure fire way not to see Judi. Rob had offered to tell Judi I was waiting to talk with her, and he had walked off to do so but never returned. So I waited. And Waited. After a while I went into the back to browse books. I could hear the phone ringing and Judi talking away in her office. Again and again, the phone rang and Judi would answer in her perkiest voice, "This is *A Better World*! Judi speaking!" Then she would lapse into conversation punctuated periodically with nearly hysterical laughter. This went on and on, and I suddenly realized that I had to put more money in the parking meter. When I came back, the door to Judi's office was wide open and I could see just inside – a little starling! I don't know where you're from, but where I grew up starlings are considered to be a very low life form. They are very noisy and so dirty that a lingering flock of them can literally ruin a neighborhood. Cities have paid big money to experts to rid themselves of these horrors. Anyway, the so-called "special" bird was just making annoying noises and scattering food; nothing special. When I went out to see where Judi was, Rob, who had returned, just said, "She's not here." So I left.

Fast forward a few months. I had been hired by Jim and Judi to build a deck and put in some sliding glass doors on their second floor. I knew that Peepers was up there and I was worried that I might freak him (because by now he was "he") out with the screaming of my Skil Saw; yet it was unavoidable. I put off working near the bird for as long as possible, but eventually got to the point where I had to begin cutting right outside Peep's window. SCREECH!!! ZZIIINNG!!! It was horrible! But you know what? That little bird just loved it! "Screech!!! Zziiinng!!!" he called back. It blew my mind! Rather, I thought it was blown. But Peeps was just getting started.

Every so often as I worked, the phone would ring. Then the answering machine would pick up, and Judi's *"Better World* message" would play. I supposed Judi had left the volume on the machine turned up because each call someone would leave a message, some of them fairly long and complicated, some featuring the same dopey laughter I had heard back at *A Better World*. So I assumed it was the same friend who had called that day calling again and again, teasing Judi. In fact, I actually recognized a couple of the callers' voices, and I knew them to be funny guys. This went on all day, unabated. I wasn't really listening, but it was loud and I couldn't help but overhear.

The next day, I had occasion to be looking at Peeps as "the phone rang", the "message" ran, and "the caller" "left a message". I about dropped over dead! IT WAS PEEPS!! I mean, THE WHOLE FREAKING THING WAS PEEPERS!!! THERE WAS NO FREAKING ANSWERING MACHINE, at ALL! That FREAKING BIRD was doing all the sound effects and all of the voices. And as

73

if that wasn't enough, it hit me as I listened that the "messages" "left by" "the callers" changed every time, but THEY ALWAYS MADE SENSE!

Paul Stangeland is a philosopher and poet. He was the editor and life support of a local magazine *"Poetry Conspiracy"*.

Mr. Peepers or "Miss Peeps", as we originally knew him, was one of the many delightful assets we came to love about visiting *The Better Worlde* Galleria. I absolutely loved going for sweets, seeing our friends perform, dancing, reading, playing with all the great puppets, stuffed animals, leggos, puzzles, and marveling over all the exquisitely beautiful works of art, crafts, paintings and clothes! Mr. Peepers, however, was by far the most fun and exciting motivation for me at the age of six. I didn't have any pets at the time but always wanted to have a bird like him.

I'll never forget the first time I met Mr. Peepers in the office area. I was wearing my favorite baseball cap, which had a bright, yellow sunflower print. Mr.

Peepers was in his big, white birdcage, nervously digging up the shredded newspaper bedding on the bottom. He seemed very fidgety and was making chattering sounds. Judi opened his door and he hopped on to her hand anxiously. As soon as he was out of the cage, he looked directly at me and pecked excitedly on the under side of the brim. It felt very neat as he drummed on my hat.

Another remarkable thing I remember about Mr. Peepers was his uncanny ability to imitate not only peoples' voices, but also the sounds of machines. I'm sure he heard the answering machine enough times! Especially since it was it was right next to his cage. He could make the exact sounds of the phone ringing, the machine picking up, and Judi's voice leaving her business reply. I never knew that starlings could be such great mocking birds!

I always enjoyed visiting Mr. Peepers and giving him an excuse to get out of his cage and fly around. It always felt so cool to have him stay on my head, even when I walked around. I think he was probably the most intelligent bird I've ever met. I'm, sure he was at least the most culturally diverse bird on the planet. I can't imagine a bird that had more exposure to great literature, music, people, food and fun. I wish we could travel back in time and visit again some day. I will no doubt look forward to going there in my dreams.

Love
Valerie Hall

Valerie holds a very special place in Judi's heart. Her visits were looked forward to by both Peepers and Judi. A charming child, she has grown up beautifully.

A Better World
Performers

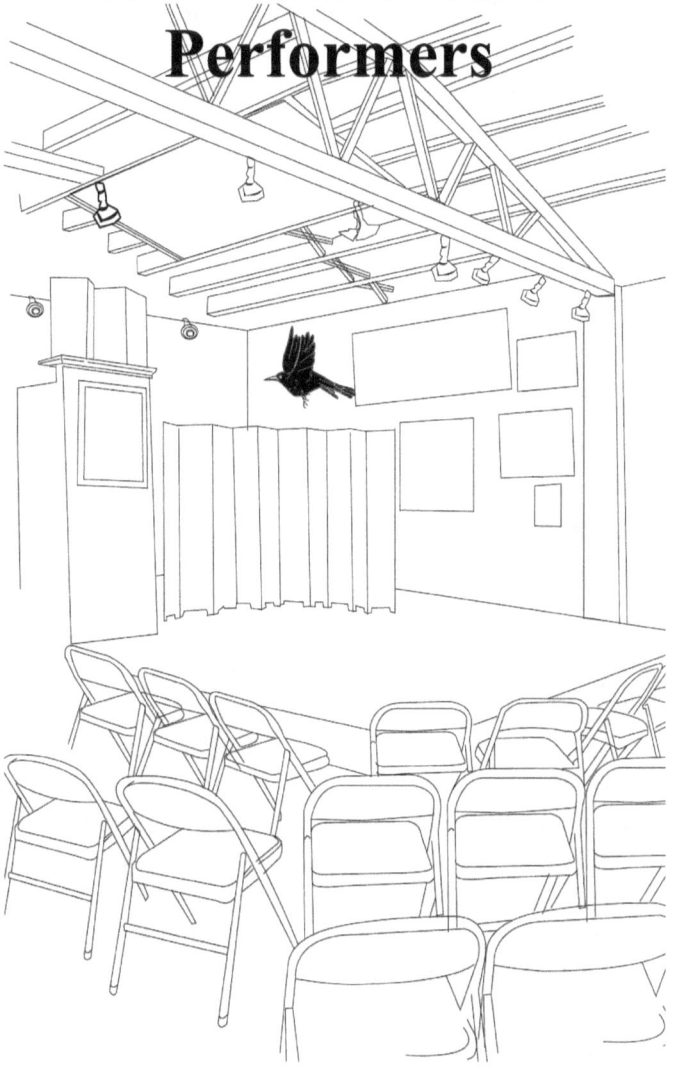

Bill Adams
Robin Adler
Irene Albrecht
Charles David Alexander
Diane Anshell
Don Attridge
Liz Axford
All Souls Day
Muriel Anderson
Greg Arriola
D.R. Auten
Charlene Baldridge
Beatriz Basile
The Beattitudes
Jim Beggs
Dave Beldock
Elithe Belofsky
Fred Benedetti
Irina Bendetsky
Cindy Lee Berryhill
Bruce Betz
Gunnar Biggs
Paul Binkley
Mike Bogle
Phillip Mycheal Bonds
Bordertown
Robin Huw Bowen
Allison Brown
Rosemary Butler
Bill Butler
California Guitar Trio
Kate Campbell
Karen Capaldi
Carlos and Terry

Jon Carmen
Anna B. Carson
Gilbert Castellanos
Diane Cawood
Cedar and Rosewood
Celtic Ensemble
Peggy Claire
Stephen Clark
Trevor Clarke
Douglas Clegg
Chris "Zooman" Clobber
Complete Expressions
Rebecca Conley
Kevin Connolly
Dan Connor
Dana Cooper
Vicky Cottle
A.J. Croce
Catie Curtis
Cusan Tan
Mark Danisofsky
Charles David
Mark Decerbo & Bob Tedde
Livy Delafield
Del Bangle
Kathi Diamont
Renata di Pietro
Mary Dolan
Pat Donahue
Cynthia Douglas
Barry Dow
Mark Dresser
Doyle Dykes
Jim Earp

Hank Easton
Cliff Eberhardt
El Pollito
Karen Elaine
Electrocarpathians
Mary Ann Escamilla
Catherine Espinosa
Renato Estacio
Lou Fanucchi
John Flood
Rosie Flores
The Flowers
Joe Foss
Juanita Franco
John Gabriel
Clara Gallagher
Jane Gardner
Harlynne Geisler
Hollis Gentry
Edward Gerhard
Patty Ghandi
Maggie Gillette
Steve Gillette
Sherry Glaser
Sallye Graves
Joseph Graziose
Richard Green
Stephanie Guderman
Doug Hall
Hand to Mouth
Joy Eden Harrrison
Calman Hart
Martin Hayes
Caroline Hazeldine

Lisa Healy
Florence Hechtel-Graziose
Peggie Howerton
Robin Henkel
Carolyn Hester
Dan Hicks
Linda Hill
Sam Hinton
Howard Horowitz
Ron Horvitz
Elizabeth Hummel
Jon Ims
Andy Irvine
Jackstraws
Deborah Liv Johnson
Art Johnson
Ellen Johnson
Holly Jones
Lawrence Juber
Kalamar
Scott Kalechstein
Paul Kamanski
Amy Lynn Kanner
John Katchur
Phil Kaufman
Eric Keeling
Kevin Kelly
Larry Keough
Barbara Kessler
Scarlet Keyes
King's Road
Bob Klymkowych
Judy Knoll
Kristen Korb

Tony Karasek
Steve Kritzer
Richard La Forge
La Jolla Renaissance Singers
James Leland
Shawn Loescher
Tom Long
Sylvia Lorraine
Vera Lukomsky
Bill Macpherson
Mandolin Madness
Robert Mann
Turiya Mareya
Lisa Martinez-Archibeque
Patty McAfee
Melissa McCrackan
Debra Mclaren
Kingsly Mclaren
Gale McNeeley
Michael McNevin
Men of Flamenco
Joe Mersch
Melissa Morgan
Bill Morrisey
Nashville Songwriters
Association
Mike Nelson
Bill Nolan
Michael O'Neal
Steve O'Connor
Theresa and Carlos Oliva
Mario Olivares
Kristina Olsen
Mick Overman
Salvador Padilla
Gregory Page

Sue Palmer
Beverly Park
Ellis Paul
Harold Payne
Jeff Pekarek
Chuck Perrin
Patric Petrie
Poetry Conspiracy
Cici Porter
Tom Prasada-Rao
Chris Prim
Janie Prim
Chris Proctor
Peter Pupping
Joel Rafael
Raggle Taggle
Laura Ravine
Preston Reed
Readers Theatre
Jean Ringgold
Rick Ruskin
Herman Salerno
Rick Saxton
Harriet Schecter
Paco Sevilla
Martin Sexton
Randy Sharp
Rick Shea
Cozy Sheridan
Gary Shiebler
Rob Shin
Keely &Preston Simms
Patricia Minton Smith
Charles Sones
Merja Soria

Peter Sprague
Delene St. Clair
Jana Stanfield
James Lee Stanley
Yale Strom
Jeanne Sutherland
George Svoboda
Phil Tabor
Barry and Holly Tashian
David Taylor
Lisa Taylor
Earl Thomas
Richard Tibbitts
Peter Tork (Monkees)
Anse Underhill
Larry Val Dumlao
Roberto Valdez
Chris Vita
Michael Waite
Donna Walker
Kerry Warren
Linda Waterfall
Peggy Watson
Ralph Waxman
Susan Werner
Robert Wetzel
Cheryl Wheeler
Erica Wheeler
Loie Wheeler
Jennifer Whisper
Steve White
Dar Williams
Paul Williams

Christopher Williams
Kelly Wilson
Lisa Wilson
Diane Winterton
Susan Wright
Yaelisa
James and Jack Young
John Zahody
Robert Zelickman
Radin Zenkl

The PRINCE and the POOPER

Written By
Judi Willkins Sarkisian
Illustrated By
Clifford Smith

The PRiNCE and the POOPER

Written By
Judi Willkins Sarkisian
Illustated By
Clifford Smith

Once upon a time in a nearby kingdom, there lived a funny little prince named Trevor. Prince Trevor had very nice parents, King James and Queen Judith. They were nice to look at and very nice to be with. So they were busy all the time with other Kings and Queens and royal things. This meant Prince Trevor had a lot of time to play around the castle and have fun with his castle friends.

The King and Queen were going to have a big party. Their favorite dish to serve at royal parties was the very famous "ten and twenty blackbirds, baked in a pie". Of course, the birds were not really baked at all and that is why "when the pie was opened the birds began to sing," fly about and do other silly things.

Clancy the cook had gone to the palace roof to collect some singing blackbirds. The King and Queen had been giving a lot of parties and Clancy found that all of the blackbirds had flown away... to less bothersome places. So he gathered ten and twenty starlings instead. One of the starlings happened to be the mother of a very noisy baby starling who was really upset at being left in the nest. Yellow beak open wide, the baby starling began to PEEP, PEE-E-EP, PEE-E-EEEP."

About this time, Prince Trevor was playing along the roof, looking for hiding places where he could spy on the Lords and Ladies. He loved to jump out and cry "BOO," when it was least expected.

"BOO! BOO-O-O-O!"

He practiced his scariest booing.

"PEEP, PEEP"

"BOO"

"PEEP, PEEP, PEE-E-E-P"

"Hey," said Prince Trevor, looking around, "who is that playing games with me." He followed the sound of the "PEEP" and soon came to the baby starling.

Prince Trevor was a mischievous fun maker, that is for sure. But he was also good and kind. He looked around for the baby bird's mother, but he couldn't find her anywhere. After several hours of loud PEEPING, he knew he would have to find the baby bird something to eat.

Prince Trevor put the noisy baby starling in his pocket and went to find Clancy the cook, who always knew what was good to eat. But Clancy was kind of grumpy; he was having a hard time getting the starlings to stay in the pie. "Go find the gardener," he growled. "Gardeners know about what to feed birds, not cooks."

Prince Trevor liked Geraldine the gardener, she was certain to know what a baby bird would eat. "Worms," that's what birds eat," Geraldine said, seeming quite pleased that she knew the answer to the young prince's question. She even knew right where the best worms were. Pretty soon all the King's gardeners were busy finding worms for the hungry, peeping little starling. They were pleased to see the little bird grow and helped Prince Trevor add berries and other good things to the orphan's diet.

Raising a baby bird is a lot of work. Prince Trevor had no idea how often and how much they like to eat! Every time the bird peeped he wanted to be fed. And every time he peeped, he pooped! The Prince named his bird "Peeps, the Pooper." King James had to hire a new servant to follow the Prince and Peeps the Pooper around, just to keep things clean. Even Prince Trevor, who loved Peeps very much, was thinking it would be nice when Peeps could fly away and poop in the sky.

That day had finally arrived. The little starling had big bird feathers instead of fuzzy baby feathers and had begun to fly around the Prince's room. Prince Trevor was going to return the starling to the castle roof. That morning, Prince Trevor was sitting with Peeps the Pooper, holding him close to his cheek and he told him for the last time.

"I love you very much."

"I love you very much," answered the starling.

The little Prince dropped the bird, and called for his father and mother. How could this be? How could this little bird possibly talk?

The King and Queen came in, very excited about the news. A talking bird must mean something very good.

The King held the bird to his face and said, "I love you very much. "

"I love you very much, much, much," answered Peeps and plopped a big poop on the king's shoe.

Prince Trevor held his breath. His father was very particular about his clothes and especially his shoes. But when the King's servant bent down to wipe the poop off of the king's shoe, he let out a big, "WOW!"

"WOW?" asked King James.

He had never thought of bird poop as "wow".

"Yech" maybe, or "icky," but never "wow".

When the servant stood up, he had a big diamond in his hand and a smile that was even bigger. The diamond in the King's favorite ring had fallen off and was sitting right where Peeps had pooped.

King James was extremely happy. This was a doubly good omen; a talking bird had saved his favorite diamond! He turned around to everyone and said, "From this day forward, the talking starling - Peeps the Pooper - shall have a home in this castle." Jokingly, he added, "and I also order everyone to look wherever Peeps poops before cleaning it up!"

Queen Judith knew the king was joking about the poop. Prince Trevor knew he was joking about the poop, but somehow, the servants did not know the king was joking about looking around wherever the starling pooped.

In no time at all, so many lost things were found, the castle had to have a new "Lost and Found Department." Because... everyone was looking wherever Peeps pooped and wherever was everywhere, because as Prince Trevor would be sure to tell you...starlings poop a lot!

Just for You..........
Playing with Peeps.

See if you can help Clancy the cook find his ten and twenty starlings to put in the pie.

You can help Peep
find his way back home.

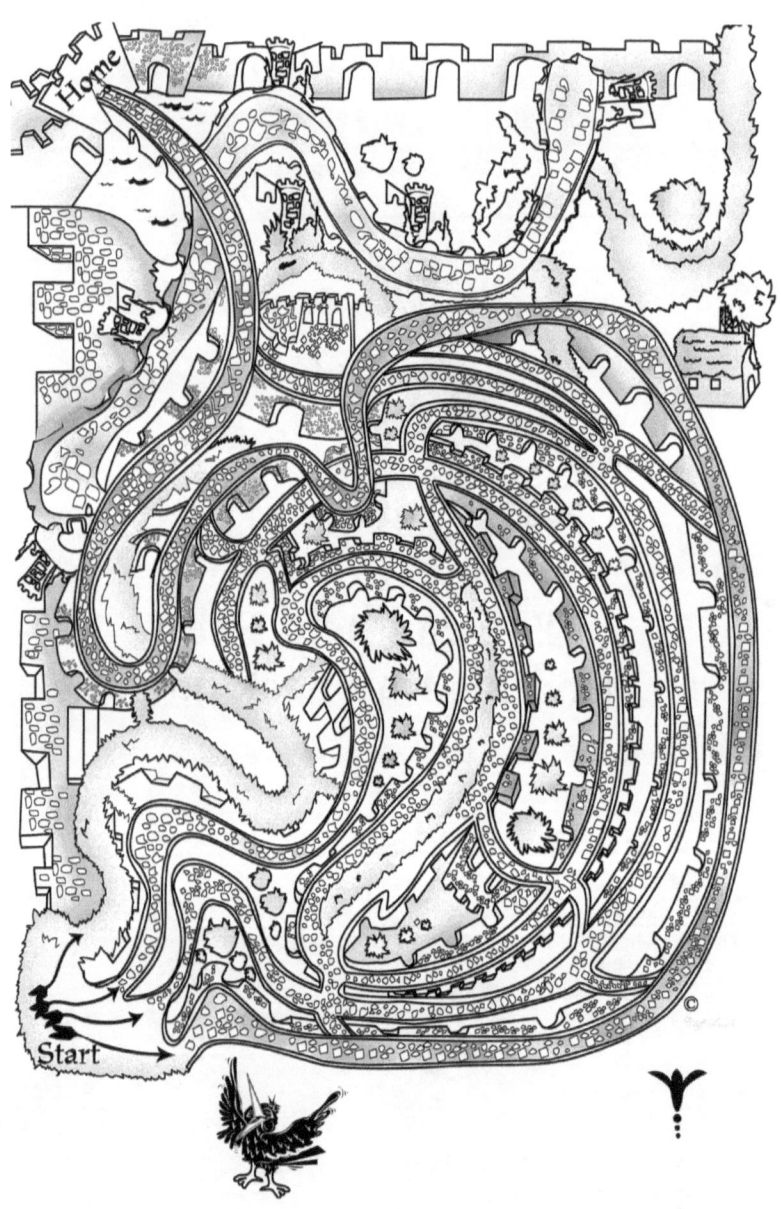

Try your hand at
drawing your favorite
creatures in this story,
"The Prince and the Pooper"

See if you can you draw Prince Trevor.

Draw here....

See if you can draw Peeps the Pooper.

Draw here....

See if you can draw Geraldine the gardener.

 Draw here....

Can you find in this word jumble
the words that are in this story
"The Prince and the Pooper"?

AFJGKRIDNFKGJYNGFGM(PRINC)EROTIYGKHJFJGKRIDI
CLIFFKGMRKTTOEWPLSDKDMFDDLEPESSDQFLRJUD
FJSNDMEIRUTHGYFJKINGFKROEPRQTLFOFKGITJYALS
PRINCEFNS.DLFGMHJBNNKHITORKFMRGTHKYLTORP
YTRRBOTSLFGKHOTPYPOIUYTREWASDFGPEEEEPPEE
FASDFGHJKLMNBVCXCLANCYMBKNLGFORKTJYNGJH
QWERTYUIOPASDFGHJKLMNBVCXZQWERFDSAZXCV
AFJGKRIDNFKGJYNGFGMTFOWEPROTIYGKHJFJGKRID
FJSNDMEIRUTHGYFJKINGFKROEPRRTLFOFKGITJYALS
QUEENPOIUYTREWQASDFGHJKLPKOJIHUGYFTDRSE/
QAWZSEXDRCFTVGYBHUNJIMKOPEEPINGLKOJIHUG\
TYRUEIWOGERALDINEFOKGITJYUHBMNVCXSDFERG1
FJSNDMEIRUTHGYFJKINGFKROEPR;TLFOFKGITJYALSH
JHUGYTFRDESDIAMONDRINGPOIUYTREWQASDFGH.
POIUYTREWQASDFGHJKL,MNBVCXZASDFGHJKIUYTF
FJSNDMEIRUTHGYFJKINGFKROEPRETLFOFKGITJYALS
FASDFGHJKLMNBVCXCLANCYMBKNLGFORKTJYNGJH
QUEENPOIUYTREWQASDFGHJKLPKOJIHUGYFTDRSE/
CLIFFKGMRKTTOEWPLSDKDMF,DLEPES.D;FLRJUDIDP
JUDISARKISIANPOIUYTREWQASDFGHJKLMNBVCXZQ
PRINCEPOIUYTREWQASDFGHJKLMNBVCXZZSEXDRC

Goodbye to all our readers and the
Peepers of the world.

See you soon...

From the artist to you..

Working on this book with Judi was pure pleasure. I've always had a love for birds of all types. So in doing the drawings it was much like watching these small-fathered creatures in my back yard. I will never know a friend like Peepers, but in this book it gave me a sense that I had known Peepers for many years even though I never met him. People that hold these small babies dear are special and unique for if we had no birds we'd have no song and without songs we'd have no joy. So when you see a small-feathered friend flying over, just enjoy their love of being who they are.

Your friend,

Clifford Smith: A bird lover

A Great New Beginning

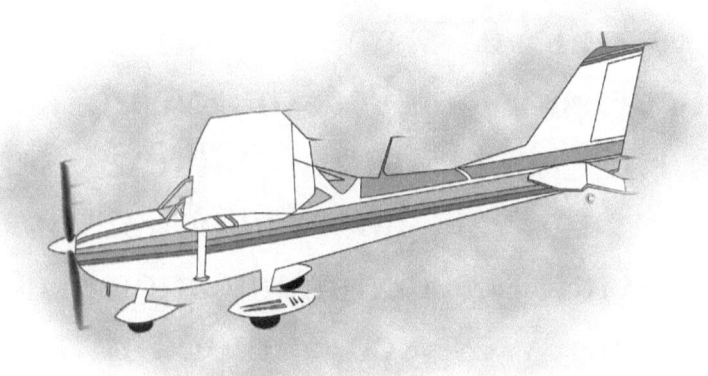

The letters and photos of Peepers had been in a folder for several years, Looking at the pictures and reading the letters made Judi too sad to write the Peepers story as she had promised. She warmed up to the project by doing a little make-believe, with the Prince and the Pooper story. Over the years she had learned about other talking starlings including a very honored pet of Mozart. It was while in communication with Dr. Meredith West (co author of "Mozart's Starling" <u>American Scientist,</u> March-April) that she decided to find a new baby starling.

Judi contacted Jackie Collins <u>www.starlingtalk.com</u> and offered to give a home to any baby that could not be reintroduced into the wild. Time (and season) went by and Judi thought it was just too much to ask for. On Sunday,

Peepers the Talking Starling

April 27, 2003, she opened an E-mail that sent her heart soaring.

Subject: Starlings

Hi Judi

I am writing to know if you are still interested in finding a baby starling. I received a note from someone in Modesto, wanting to know if anyone around her wanted one.

Sincerely, Jackie

Subject: Re: Starlings

Good Morning Jackie!

The answer is, of course, yes. The problem may be distance, as Modesto is about 7 hours from San Diego.

Thank you for remembering,

Judi Sarkisian

Subject: Re*:* Starlings

It looks like I have babies showing up everywhere. This person I had not considered when I found out how far she lives from you. It turns out she is in the aviation business and could take the baby to you. Her email is below.

I was wondering if I could get in touch with Jill (the woman in San Diego)? Maybe you could have her e-mail me, or let her know that I have a starling or two for adoption? If I don't get a response soon, I know what will happen - I'll end up keeping them all.
Thanks, Jennifer

If you could work something out. I think this would be the best solution...
Sincerely, Jackie

From: Jennifer

To: Judi

Subject: starling baby

Hi!

The logistics of getting down there may be tough-I have a friend who just bought a nice, fast, twin engine plane (actually he is a former student of mine) and recently I was in San Diego - it was in little under three hours there, and five hours back (due to winds). He would LOVE to take me down there again. The problem is the thing burns close to 30 gallons per hour, at $2.60 a gallon-close to $650. If he is going there anyway, I doubt if he'll for any $$$.

On the other hand, I own a crappy (I use that term with affection) Cessna 172, and the trip would cost me $150 total. The problem, it's slow. That would be a two-day trip for me, unless you'd be willing to come up to Santa Barbara or somewhere North of L.A.

But them, my mom never gets out of the house, and I think she'd love to take an overnight trip somewhere.

What better excuse to get away?

Jennifer

To Judi, the idea of a baby starling being delivered by private plane had to have a special meaning. This bird must be meant for her. The plans went forward and on the 17th of May, Judi, Jim and Judi's sister Susan went to Montgomery Airport to await the arrival of the new Peepers. There is a great Mexican restaurant, Casa Machada, on the runway. Sitting at a window table, sipping margaritas, they watched a gold Cessna 172 taxi up right in front of their window…. More good signs!! The pilot (Jennifer) jumped from the plane, a pretty little blond who looked like a teenager. Not at all what they were expecting! Judi, Jim and Susan run from the restaurant to meet their new friends. It was love at first sight for everyone.

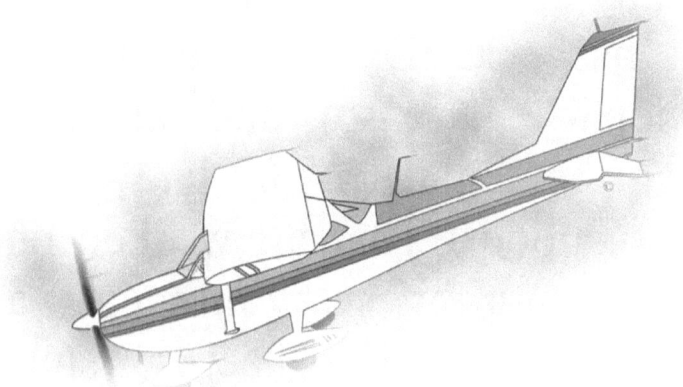

The only one who seemed a little worn by the event was Jennifer's Mother. She has COPD (Cardio Obstructive Pulmonary Disease) and at one time during the flight her P02 had dropped to 65 (not good.) That all worked out, but not without a few scary moments: a great beginning for the next Peeper's story.

About the Author

Judi Sarkisian was a professional storyteller for many years. She performed with her own company and Young Audiences as: the Fairy Godmother, the Snow Princess and Pirate Captain Morgana. She wrote the scripts and many of the stories for hundreds of shows. When she and Jim opened A Better World, her writing was mainly for advertisements and promotional material for artists. She wrote an exercise book for their medical practice, <u>Exerchair: The Exercise While You Sit in Your Chair Program</u> and co-authored Admiral Faucett's Naval Biography, <u>Memoirs of a Naval Physician</u>. Judi writes for fun and because it is still the best way to share a good story!

www.ingramcontent.com/pod-product-compliance
Lightning Source LLC
Chambersburg PA
CBHW051426280526
45785CB00003B/1172